The Wild West in American History

RIVERMEN

Written by Gail Stewart
Illustrated by Joe Nordstrom
Edited by Mark E. Ahlstrom

LIBRARY OF CONGRESS
Library of Congress Cataloging-in-Publication Data

Stewart, Gail, 1949-
    Rivermen / by Gail B. Stewart.
      p. cm. -- (The Wild West in American history)
    Summary: A history of life on the river in the United States, particularly
on the Mississippi, when rivermen, by their work, made possible exploration,
settlement, and travel not otherwise possible.
    ISBN 0-86625-409-9
    1. River life--West (U.S.)--History--19th century--Juvenile literature.
2. Inland navigation--West (U.S.)--History--19th century--Juvenile literature.
3. West (U.S.)--Description and travel--Juvenile literature. 4. Frontier and
pioneer life--West (U.S.)--Juvenile literature. [1. River life--Mississippi River
--History--19th century.] I. Title. II. Series.
F596.S85 1990
978' .009693--dc20
                                             89-37767
                                                 CIP
                                                     AC

Rourke Publications, Inc.
Vero Beach, Florida, 32964

RIVERMEN

RIVERMEN

The Old West—the very name makes us think of horses, dusty trails over the deserts and the mountains, and covered wagons. We have all seen television programs, or pictures in books, showing horse-drawn wagons full of settlers making their slow way west in the 19th century. It might be easy to assume that overland journeys were the only ways people moved from place to place. But that isn't true at all!

It is true that the first frontiersmen and trappers traveled on almost invisible little trails through forests and mountains. As the years went on, people back east heard about the wonders of the West—the forests brimming with game and the rich soil for planting. More and more people hurried to make the trip themselves, to move themselves and their households to this new, more attractive place.

Our history books are filled with the names and stories of those who led settlers westward. Daniel Boone, Kit Carson, and Jim Bridger are the most famous. Yet is is important to understand that there were other "roads" west—a whole network of them. They were the rivers of the United States.

Life on the river was both beautiful and dangerous. There were remarkable heroes and villains, just as there were on land. Those who lived and worked on the rivers of the Old West are perhaps not as well known as the other characters of the West, but their lives were just as exciting.

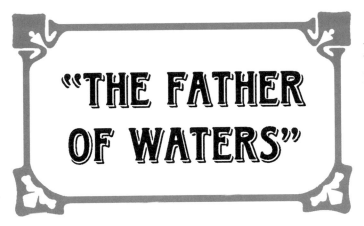

"THE FATHER OF WATERS"

The first "West" was really the territory west of the Appalachian Mountains in what is now Indiana, Kentucky, and Tennessee. The families who made the dangerous journey through the mountains cleared land and began farming on the frontier.

As their first settlements began to grow, and they had farm products to sell, they had a problem. How could they get fruits and vegetables back to the cities and towns in the East? The paths they had followed across the mountains were dangerous and quite narrow—certainly not the best route for wagonloads of farm goods.

Settlers, as well as farmers, used the Ohio River to get to the Mississippi River. *(Photo: The Filson Club.)*

These frontier farmers looked elsewhere for their markets, instead. They looked to the big, busy city of New Orleans far to the southwest. How could they get the goods to New Orleans? They used rivers—primarily the Ohio and Mississippi rivers.

The Mississippi River is the large river that cuts the Unites States from north to south. It begins as a little trickle of water up north at Lake Itasca, Minnesota. It travels more than 2,350 miles south until it empties into the Gulf of Mexico below the city of New Orleans.

The Mississippi has been called "The Father of Waters" for hundreds of years. The reason for this, of course, is that it is the heart of a huge water system. Together with the streams and rivers that empty into it, the Mississippi River drainage system is made up of more than 14,000 miles of waterways!

The frontier farmers simply built crude boats out of lumber and floated their cargo down the Ohio River to Cairo, Illinois. They let the current of the water provide the power. At Cairo, where the Ohio joins the Mississippi River, the goods were transferred to larger boats for the trip to New Orleans. The farmers would usually abandon their crude boats, and just walk home!

The Mississippi River and its main branches, the Missouri River (from the west) and the Ohio River (from the east), were more than just a way for frontier farmers to get their goods to market.

The rivers also provided a means for explorers, gold seekers, and trappers to work their way farther west. For many years, it was even thought that there was a way to get to the Pacific Ocean, by water, through North America. This would have made it easier for traders to get to the Orient, where valuable treasures, such as spices and beautiful silks, could be bought. We know now that there is no such waterway, but this "Northwest Passage," as it was called, was sought throughout the 1700's and 1800's.

"THIS RIVER GOES WHERE IT WANTS"

Early travelers on the Mississippi River had to be on a constant lookout for whirlpools—especially if they were in small boats.

*P*eople who live on the banks of a creek or river say that each river has a character of its own—almost like a personality. This is undoubtedly true of the Mississippi. The river might seem like a very calm, peaceful

body of water, but its "personality" is quite changeable.

Although it starts quite innocently in Minnesota—a person could easily walk across its source at Lake Itasca—the Mississippi grows quickly into a powerful, rushing river. The lower part of the river, flowing through Mississippi and Louisiana, might be anywhere from a half-mile to a mile across. It is in this part of the river that its great force can be seen. There are giant whirlpools and eddies that suck debris around and around to the river bottom. Logs and timber might as well be tiny sticks—they are no match for the mighty current.

The time of spring flooding is the most dangerous. The spring rains and melting snow add to the river. In some parts, the Mississippi rises more than 50 feet, spilling over its banks.

"This river goes where it wants to go," say people who have seen the Mississippi in the springtime.

In modern times, the Mississippi has been "tamed" with a system of dikes, levees, and dams. That's not the way it was in the early days of the Old West. There were no boundaries then. The lower sections of the river could expand from a mile to nearly 50 miles across!

Needless to say, farms, homes, and anything else in the river's path were often washed away. Any map of the course of the river in those days would change often, depending on the depth of the water and the strength of the current. This changeability made it hard for captains and pilots of early riverboats. Landmarks that were helpful on one trip may not even be there the next time!

THE BIG MUDDY

The Mississippi, as dangerous and unpredictable as it was, was nothing compared to the Missouri River. Called "The Big Muddy" by the early settlers because of the tons and tons of mud and silt it carries along in its water, the Missouri is the western branch of the Mississippi River. So much mud is in its water, in fact, that scientists estimate that 500 million tons of silt are carried by the Missouri into the Mississippi every year!

The river begins in southwestern Montana, continues through North and South Dakota,

and then flows along the western boundary of Iowa, Nebraska, and Missouri. At St. Louis it joins up with the Mississippi.

Like the Mississippi, the Missouri River has a personality all its own. It, too, was a highly unpredictable river, only more so. Its powerful currents were constantly carving out new shorelines and islands in the muddy water.

It was flooding that caused the most trouble. On the Missouri the flooding occurred two times every year—once in April with the spring rains, and again in June when the Rocky

During times of high water, travel on the Missouri River could be dangerous.

Mountain snowfields melted. Because of geography, flooding on the Missouri was more extreme and happened faster. The sudden flooding would cause the river to change into a roaring, brown torrent. The raging water would uproot trees and heave large rocks away from the shore. It was these underwater hazards that made travel on the Missouri so dangerous.

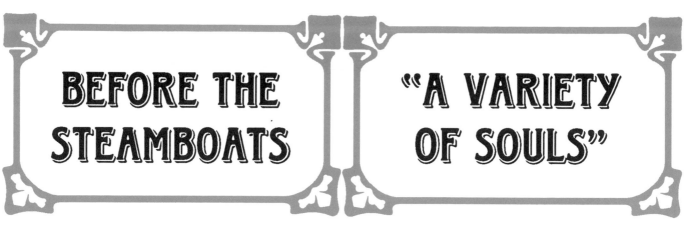

BEFORE THE STEAMBOATS

"A VARIETY OF SOULS"

The age of the steamboats was an exciting one, but it's important to remember that there was plenty of river travel before the steamboat was invented. The first boats, of course, were the canoes of the various Indian tribes. Early explorers and frontiersmen learned the design of the canoe from the Indians.

The canoe, however, had its limitations. It was fine for one or two people, and a few supplies. But the settlers needed more space—enough for boxes and crates of cargo. It was for this purpose that "flatboats" became useful.

A flatboat looked pretty much as its name suggests. It was actually a raft, with a few improvements. Flatboats were anywhere from 15 to 50 feet long, and between 12 and 20 feet wide. They were squared off in the bow (the front) and in the stern (the back). A good deal of the boat was roofed—this protected the cargo, as well as the passengers.

Flatboats on the Mississippi, Ohio, and Missouri rivers were good only for going downstream. They were propelled by the current, although they could be steered somewhat. There was a 50-foot-long oar in the stern that was pushed either right or left as a means of controlling the direction of the boat.

No one could ever accuse a flatboat of being speedy. Depending on the current and the obstacles encountered on the journey, a flatboat trip from St. Louis to New Orleans would take about four months. Obviously, perishable goods such as fruits and vegetables would have to be sold much closer to home!

Since they were downstream vehicles only, how did the owner get his boat back upstream? The answer is simple—he didn't. After reaching its destination, the flatboat was torn up and the timber was sold. After selling the timber and the cargo, the owner traveled back home either on foot or by another type of boat—one that could travel upstream.

Flatboatmen were not all farmers taking their harvest to market, although many of them did just that. Some were travelers, on their way to a new home in a new place. These people were content to let the current move along wherever it wanted to take them.

There were also a number of flatboats that were a lot like houseboats. They were home to families who simply enjoyed life on the river. They fished, trapped, and stopped whenever they felt like it. They usually began their journey in the spring in the North. By fall, when the weather turned cold, they had traveled far enough south that they were warm and comfortable. They usually spent the winter fishing on the lower part of the Mississippi River. When spring came, they might sell their flatboat and book passage on a keelboat that was headed upstream to the Ohio or Missouri rivers. Then they would begin the voyage all over again.

Among the flatboatmen, too, were many professionals. They made a living transporting cargo on the rivers. These men were knowledgeable in the ways of a river. They understood how to navigate around sandbars, and how to avoid underwater hazards. These professional flatboatmen were a rowdy crew. They enjoyed their river life, and they passed the days on the boat singing, telling stories, and dancing. There was usually a fiddle-player aboard, and this member of the crew was allowed to "play hooky" from his duties. The rest of the crew would rather have music while they worked than an extra pair of hands!

Flatboatmen often had to work hard, but along straight stretches of the river they could enjoy themselves.

This old drawing shows settlers using a
flatboat to transport their covered wagon.
(Photo: Oregon Historical Society.)

These rivermen sold their services for a pretty reasonable price—even for those days. A large flatboat could be rented, crew and all, for a mere $2 a day! Even after steamboats appeared on the river in the early 1800's, many farmers who couldn't afford steamboat prices continued to hire flatboatmen to take their cargoes to market.

HEADING UPSTREAM AND DOWN

and it did what a flatboat simply couldn't—it could travel upstream, too.

The design of a keelboat was less square than that of a flatboat. A keelboat was more tapered and could move more quickly through the water. The bow and the stern were pointed. It was a large boat—most were about 60 feet long and 20 feet wide. The keelboat could carry more than 50 tons of cargo under its roofed deck.

Most keelboats had a mast and canvas sails, although they weren't used as often as you might think. The Ohio, the Missouri, and the

Trappers use a small keelboat to bring a load of furs down the Missouri River. (Photo: Denver Public Library. Western History Dept.)

Besides the flatboat, there was another boat on the river before the coming of the steamboat. It was called a "keelboat,"

Mississippi are such crooked rivers that there was hardly time at all to hoist the sails before the river changed directions.

Like the flatboat, the keelboat had an easy time going downstream with the current. The tricky part, however, was heading upstream. Most of the power for a keelboat heading upstream was supplied by the muscles of the crew. There were three ways (besides the sail) of powering the keelboat.

The first was by rowing. If the current happened to be rather light in a section of the river, the crew members would use oars. There were three or four pairs of oars. The man who was lucky enough to be in charge just sat on top of the roof and made sure the rowers kept in rhythm.

The most common way of propelling a keelboat in shallow water was by poling. Five or six men would stand in a line on either side of the bow, each one holding a long wooden pole. Each man would push the pole into the water and walk back to the rear of the boat, holding onto the pole as he walked. The boat would be pushed

forward (hopefully in a straight line) as long as each line of men was pushing as hard as the other. When the line of men reached the stern of the boat, the men would walk quickly back to the front and begin again.

Sometimes, however, the water was too deep for poling, or the current was too strong, or there were snags or other obstacles in the river. In that case, the men would use a long rope (sometimes over 1,000 feet long), called a "cordelle." The cordelle was fastened to the keelboat on one end. The other end was pulled by several of the

One of the most dreaded jobs on the river was having to use a "cordelle" to pull a boat upstream. It was back-breaking work.

men. Sometimes the men sludged through the muddy river water, waist-deep or even neck-deep. Other times, if the current was too strong for men to stand, they would pull the boat from the river bank. Towing, or "cordelling," was a slow and agonizingly painful process. Rivermen who worked on keelboats often had raw, bleeding hands from the rough rope.

"HALF-HORSE, HALF-ALLIGATOR"

$\mathcal{K}$eelboatmen were a breed unlike any other. Because of the muscle involved in their work, they considered themselves superior to anyone else on the river—or anywhere else, for that matter! They strutted around, puffing out their chests and showing their biceps to anyone who would notice. They were, it is true, a brave and talented bunch—they certainly had to be to strong-arm their way up the Western rivers.

The men who worked on keelboats enjoyed drinking, swearing, and bragging. They loved

making up long-winded speeches about themselves and their accomplishments. For instance, one might say, "I'm Bill Miller, and I'm the meanest, foulest, toughest wildcat this side of the Ohio River. I can out-drink, out-shoot, and out-dance any mother's son on this river!"

Bill would go on and on, yelling and cursing and bragging in the most colorful way he could think of. It wasn't so much what the words meant as how they sounded, and the rhythm they made. In that way, keelboatman-talk isn't too different from a lot of the street talk in some of our cities today!

Besides bragging and drinking, keelboatmen occasionally amused themselves by getting into incredibly dirty fights. The object was usually to gouge an eye out with a thumb, or to use one's teeth to bite off the other fellow's ear or the tip of his nose. As hard as it may be to believe, all of these things happened!

Keelboatmen entertained one another by bragging about how tough they were.

Mike Fink, the legendary keelboatman, used to amuse himself and his fellow boatmen with some unusual target practice!

The most famous keelboatman of them all was a man named Mike Fink. So much has been written about him, in so many variations, that it is hard to tell what is fact and what is purely legend. He was, like other keelboatmen, a braggart and a fighter. Mike used to say about himself, "I'm Mike Fink, half-horse and half-alligator. Hurray for me! I'm a land screamer, I'm a snapping turtle, I'm chock full o' fight. I can out-run, out-dive, out-jump, out-holler, and out-lick any white thing in the shape o' human that's ever put foot within two thousand miles o' the big Mississippi!"

Mike Fink, it was said, could go on in this way—without repeating himself at all—for more than 30 minutes! He was also supposed to have been the best shot on the river. It was said that even after drinking a gallon of whiskey, he could shoot the tail off a pig 90 paces away! He enjoyed nothing more than to have friends help him with his target practice. Mike would do it in the style of William Tell, with a friend balancing a small object on his head. Mike would take aim and fire, and the friend would sigh with relief when Mike hit the target.

There are several versions of the way Mike died in 1822. One popular story is that he and

a friend were both in love with the same woman. The friend agreed to a round of target practice, and balanced a little cup of whiskey on his head. Mike, having been drinking more than even he was used to, counted off several paces and fired, hitting his rival between the eyes. "Son of a gun, man, you spilled the whiskey," Mike scolded the dead man. The man's brother is said to have then jumped up and shot Mike in the heart, killing him instantly.

THE AGE OF STEAM

*T*he keelboats and their crews were doomed, however. As steamboats became more and more common on the Ohio, the

Mississippi, and the Missouri, it was clear that the days of the keelboat were numbered. Muscle and strength, no matter how interesting and colorful, simply couldn't compete with the amazing new boats that could carry hundreds of times more cargo (and passengers) in a fraction of the time.

The Indians called them *Pelenore*, meaning "fire canoe." Others thought they looked a lot like wedding cakes, with their many layers of white columns and arches. Whatever they looked like, they dominated the Western rivers—and the towns on their banks—for most of the 19th century.

The steamboat came to the Western rivers years after it had been introduced to the rivers of the East. The reason was, simply, the depth of the water. Robert Fulton, the man responsible for building the first really practical working steamboat, intended it to be used on the deep, rather calm waters of the Hudson River in New York. Rivermen on the Ohio, the Missouri, and the Mississippi laughed at the idea of a steamboat tackling their rivers. They were all too familiar with what the savage currents and whirlpools could do to a boat.

With good reason, people thought the new steamboats had the look of a wedding cake.

MAKING A NEW STEAMBOAT

By 1811, however, steamboats were operating on the Mississippi, and soon after on other Western rivers. The design was changed, of course. Any steamboat that ran on the wild Western rivers had to have less "draw"—that is, it had to sit higher in the water. None of the rivers in the West was deep enough to be safe for a deep-hulled boat like the steamboats of the East.

One of the people who had a lot to do with modifying the steamboat to fit the rivers of the West was a man called Henry Shreve. He built a boat called the *Enterprise*, which was very much like an Eastern steamboat. He saw immediately, however, that it wouldn't be right for the Mississippi. It constantly ran aground. He built a second boat in 1816, called the *Washington*, on which he made several changes. The first was to put a deck over the hull of his

The *Rosebud* carried people and cargo on the Missouri River. *(Photo: University of Oklahoma.)*

boat. He moved the boilers, which were used to create steam, onto the deck. Above this deck, he built a second deck for passengers. Shreve also changed the old Fulton steamboat engine. He wanted one that was lighter and less bulky. His new engine produced more power than the old engine, and this was important. Boats fighting currents on the Mississippi and Missouri, especially, had to have lots of power.

The *Washington* proved itself to be a good design for travel on Western rivers, and other boat makers began to imitate Shreve's design.

Shreve made another important contribution to Western steamboat travel. Aware that there would be far more traffic on the Western rivers, Shreve knew that something had to be done about the "snags," or uprooted trees. There were thousands of them, lying in the water waiting to wreck an unsuspecting ship.

Shreve built a "snag boat," an odd-looking boat whose job it was to remove snags from the river. The boat had a forked hull, with special equipment in the front for lifting heavy logs and debris out of the water. When a snag was pulled out of the water, it could be chopped into small, harmless pieces. The pieces were then allowed to float back into the river!

Shreve and his snag boat, the *Heliopolis*, were kept busy by the government for many years on the Mississippi River. The spot in Louisiana where Shreve and his crew made their headquarters eventually became a town, then a large city. Today, the city—Shreveport, Louisiana—bears his name!

Henry Shreve designed and built the first snag boat. It proved to be very useful for making travel on the river safer.

THE WESTERN STEAMBOAT

By 1849 there were more than 1,000 steamboats in operation on the rivers of the West. Many of these were small boats, carrying cargo (sometimes more than 200 tons of it) and mail, as well as a few passengers. Some of the steamboats, however, were large, luxurious craft, almost like hotels on water.

Although there were some differences between steamboats, they all ran in pretty much the same way. There were boilers—often as many as 12—that needed to be constantly fueled. The heat produced by the fire in the boilers created steam, and this steam turned the paddle wheel.

Some boats had a stern wheel, which means that there was a single paddle wheel located in the back of the ship. Other boats had two wheels, one on each side. There were a couple of advantages to two-wheeled boats—they were faster, and they were easier to steer. On the other hand, the stern-wheeler was often preferred by captains on the Missouri, for it was easier to control in shallow water and in narrow channels.

The fuel for the boats was either coal or wood. The boats couldn't carry all the fuel they needed for a long trip, of course, so there were plenty of stops along the way. Many farmers along the river had woodpiles ready to sell to the crew of any steamboat that happened along. Often, nighttime stops were necessary. Farmers who had wood to sell listened for the steamboat whistle, and hurried to light a bonfire by the riverbank. The fire would alert the steamboat captain that there was fuel available.

SEVEN KINDS OF SOUP!

The fanciest steamboats on Western rivers, and the biggest ones, were found on the Mississippi. (The Missouri was simply too wild and rough for a large luxury steamboat to travel on safely.) The Mississippi steamboats were often astonishing in their size. One boat, the *Eclipse*, was 350 feet long!

In addition to their larger size, these Mississippi steamboats had many comforts to offer their passengers. While the Missouri steamboats had no running water or heat, some of the elegant Mississippi craft had large staterooms, with thick carpeting and plenty of room. Some boats had lovely dining rooms, decorated with velvet and crystal. Large chandeliers hung from the ceilings.

The food, too, was elegant on some of these boats. One museum has several menus from steamboats—and they could rival the menus of any expensive modern restaurant. One steamboat kitchen offered 15 different types of meat, 7 kinds of soup, and 13 fancy desserts!

This was pretty high living, when you consider that the passengers paid only a penny per mile for their fares.

All steamboats, like this stern-wheeler, had to make frequent stops for fuel.

No one—not even the captain—could tell the pilot how to navigate the steamboat.

THE CREW

No matter what the size of the boat, a large and capable crew was needed to keep it running smoothly. The head of the steamboat was the captain. He was the absolute authority when it came to matters of cargo, machinery, fuel, and so on. When there was a problem with a passenger, or with the food supply in the boat kitchen, it was up to the captain to set things right.

Once the boat pulled away from the dock, however, the real authority took over. He was called the pilot, and he sat—or stood—on the very top of the boat, in the pilothouse. There was no one who could give orders to a steamboat pilot when the boat was moving, not even the

captain. That was the law. The pilot had total command of the direction, the speed, and the solutions to any problems of navigation that came up during the journey.

The importance of the pilot was reflected in how he was paid. The pilot of a Mississippi steamboat earned twice or three times what his captain earned. On the Missouri River, because of the difficulty of a pilot's job, he earned six times as much as his captain.

One of the reasons a pilot's job was so difficult was that so much depended on his memory. He had to memorize the sandbars, the areas where snags were lurking, and where the rapids were. He needed to make split-second decisions,

depending on the depth of the water, or a change in the weather. Not only the safety of his boat and cargo, but also the lives of the passengers and crew depended on his memory and his good eyes.

There were more crew members than the pilot and the captain, however. There were engineers and firemen, whose job it was to keep the boilers burning hot. There were deckhands and stewards. There were roustabouts—strong, muscle-bound men who had to load and unload cargo at every stop. In addition to these crew members, there were cooks, waiters, and sometimes even a band, if the boat was large enough!

Most steamboat crews—from the pilot and captain on down—loved speed. Safety was important, but, unfortunately, it was often secondary to speed. When the pilot saw another boat nearby, or when he was reasonably sure that a stretch of safe water lay before them, he would give the signal for more speed. A race—with or without an opponent—was what made steamboating exciting.

Frequently, the order was given to the firemen and engineers to "throw in anything that'll burn." Wood, coal, furniture, even bacon grease—anything that would make the fire burn faster and hotter—was thrown into the boilers!

It was the coming of the railroad to the West that soon put an end to the great era of the steamboat.

THE END OF AN ERA

$\mathcal{T}$he steamboats, like the keelboats before them, finally became almost extinct. Railroads, which had been gradually creeping westward, proved to be more reliable and faster for passengers and cargo. By the 1880's, there weren't enough customers to keep the steamboats in business. The towns and cities that had been thriving because of the steamship business had to look away from the river for their survival.

Some of the smaller steamboats continued to work on the rivers, hauling supplies for government workers building dams. Some steamboats were used to carry coal or push lumber down from the lumber camps in the northern woods. In recent times, a few steamboats have been fixed up just as they were in their prime—painted, scrubbed, and polished. These boats now carry tourists and sightseers up and down the Mississippi.

Western rivers aren't as wild as they once were. Government engineers have built dams, removed some of the snags, and paved some of the banks. The rivers of the West, however, are still fascinating to many people who know about the contribution the early rivermen made to the American West.

DANGERS ON THE RIVER

*T*here were dangers—thousands of them—that made life miserable for captains of the riverboats (as well as the passengers) on Western rivers in the 19th century.

For one thing, a river is filled with sand bars, unexpected shallow places in the middle of very deep water. Such sand bars were responsible not only for delays, but also for dangerous accidents on the river. Boats hitting a sand bar would be seriously damaged, and would often sink.

As a result of flooding, there would be real hazards lurking, unseen, in the water—hazards that spelled danger to riverboats. One such danger was called a "snag." A snag was a clump of trees that had been uprooted in a flood. The trees would float out into the middle of the river, where their roots would take hold of the muddy bottom. A heavy snag could easily rip the bottom out of a riverboat.

A "sawyer" was a hazard much like a snag, except harder to see. Instead of its roots sinking to the bottom of the river, a sawyer was "hooked" onto another branch, and would bob up and down in the water. A steamboat captain might look ahead and see clear, open water when the sawyer was below the surface. Then, when it was too late to veer around it, the sawyer would slowly swing to the surface. Many steamboats on both the Mississippi and Missouri rivers went down because of sawyers.

Western rivers flowed through territory that could be extremely uncomfortable for travelers, and often downright frightening. In the summer the banks buzzed with thick, black clouds of mosquitoes. Passengers on a slow-moving boat were easy victims for these hungry insects—and these were the days before sprays and repellents.

The paths of the Western rivers passed through areas that are a weather-forecaster's nightmare. Violent storms, complete with thunder, lightning, and tornadoes, would come out of nowhere, making it necessary for the boat captain to try to find some safe place to stop.

Besides the natural dangers of the river and the climate, those who traveled by boat faced other hardships. The valleys through which the rivers ran were home to a number of tribes of Native Americans, such as the Pawnee, the Sioux, and the Blackfoot. Many of these tribes were hostile to the white settlers. They viewed the boatloads of people as enemies, coming to invade their land. It was not uncommon for an armed band of Indians to attack a boat that was stopped or slowed down for some reason.

Tragedy was a big part of the age of the steamboat. The average "life expectancy" of a steamboat on the Mississippi or the Missouri in the 19th century was only five or six years. Boats hit snags and sank. They were torn apart by ice or even high winds. All of these were costly in terms of property and occasionally of human life—but none were as feared as a steamboat fire.

Fire was a danger anytime a steamboat pilot put safety aside and tried to outrun another boat, or tried to make better time. The boilers could only handle so much pressure without exploding.

The engineers and firemen didn't have the precise dials and controls with which boilers of today are equipped. The engineers did it all by listening, hoping that their ears would tell them when a boiler was reaching its full capacity. There were all too many times, however, when the listening method just didn't work—or, worse, when the captain or pilot ordered the crew to ignore their ears and keep fueling the fires.

There were hundreds of boiler explosions. They were gruesome, bloody accidents. Damage from the explosions wasn't limited to the boat, either. Nearby towns and farms often sustained damage from flying debris and sparks. When the steamer *White Cloud* exploded at a dock in St. Louis in 1849, the fire spread to 23 other steamboats. More than a dozen blocks of the city were burned to the ground.

Life on the river was full of danger!

IN THE DAYS OF THE RIVERMEN

1770	Mike Fink born in Pittsburgh, Pennsylvania.
1776	America wins independence from England.
1787	John Fitch builds the first working steamboat.
1807	Robert Fulton's steamboat, the *Clermont*, makes its first trip on the Hudson, from New York to Albany. It averages five miles per hour.
1809	James Madison sworn in as fourth president of the United States.
1810	United States population is 7,239,881.
1811	The Cumberland Road is started, enabling settlers to pass through the Appalachian Mountains.
1812	First U.S. life insurance company formed in Philadelphia.
1814	Washington, D.C., burned by British soldiers.
1814	"Star-Spangled Banner" written.
1816	Indiana joins the Union.
1818	Illinois becomes the 21st state.
1819	First steamboat crosses the Atlantic Ocean.
1821	First public high school in the United States opens its doors.
1824	John Quincy Adams elected president.
1825	Erie Canal officially opens.
1828	*Webster's Dictionary* published.
1829	America's first school for the blind opens in Boston.
1839	Official rules for baseball are written down.
1837	Elijah Lovejoy, who spoke out against slavery, is killed by a pro-slavery mob in Illinois.
1840	America's population is just over 17 million.
1852	The steamboat *Saluda* explodes near Lexington, Missouri, killing 150 people.
1853	Funds appropriated by Congress for a transcontinental railroad.
1865	Potato chips introduced in the United States by a black chef.
1887	Railroads finally take over the shipping and passenger business of the steamboats.